Infantry Tactics

Infantry Tactics

by

Anthony Farrar-Hockley

illustrated by

The County Studio

Almark Publishing Co Ltd London

First Published 1976.

ISBN 85524 255 8

Distributed in the U. S. A. by
Squadron/Signal Publications Inc.,
3515E, Ten Mile Road,
Warren, Michigan 48091.

Printed in Great Britain by
Edwin Snell Printers,
Park Road, Yeovil,
Somerset,
for the publishers, Almark Publishing Co. Ltd.
49 Malden Way, New Malden,
Surrey KT3 6EA, England.

Contents

Introduction to the Mechanics of War

Infantry Tactics by Anthony Farrar-Hockley introduces The Mechanics of War, a new series from Almark.

The first four books cover the tactics employed by the three land and the air arms during the Second World War in Europe.

Shelford Bidwell writes on Artillery, Christopher Chant on Ground Attack, and Kenneth Macksey on Tank Tactics.

They cover the neglected area of small unit tactics which are the basis of every great battle and explain how company, squadron or battery orders were passed down and carried out. The books give the reader an insight into how the historic strategic decisions of the war became the tactics of the soldier on the ground.

The Mechanics of War will follow these books with a nation by nation coverage of the uniforms, small arms, tanks and artillery used in Europe, the Mediterranean and Russia.

Each volume will show how a nation used and modified its weapons and equipment in the light of tactical experience in each campaign.

Acknowledgements

All pictures with the exception of those listed below are from the Imperial War Museum collection. Pages 14, 15, 16, 53 (top), 68 Almark. Diagrams by Eric Rose. Quotation pages 62 to 68 via United States Official History.

Britain and Germany

The British infantry went to war in 1939 with weapons and equipment developed for the most part before or during World War I. The standard personal weapon was the No 1 Short Magazine Lee-Enfield rifle of .303-inch calibre, complementary to which was the long bayonet; a combination brought into service after the Boer War as a result of Lord Roberts' recommendations. Officers and certain soldier specialists carried pre-war pattern revolver pistols. An auxiliary weapon was the No. 36 fragmentation grenade, developed during World War I from the Mills bomb.

The battalion support weapons – that is, the weapons disposed directly by the commanding officer to provide a weight of fire to assist one or more of the four rifle companies manoeuvring or in defence – had been developed as a result of experience in trench warfare. They were the 3-inch mortar and the Vickers .303-inch medium machine-gun. There were however several innovations whose production had been hastened by the belated rearmament of the United Kingdom in the 1930s.

The first of these was the Bren light machine-gun, developed by the Royal Ordnance Factory at Enfield from a Czechoslovak weapon designed at Brno – the title Bren being a composite of the first two letters of each place name. A .303 weapon, fed by a magazine charged with 28 to 30 rounds, the Bren was lighter and easier to maintain in action than the Lewis gun which it was to replace in the rifle companies of the infantry battalion. To provide the commanding officer with a further reserve of fire power, and a highly mobile one, a new platoon was added to the mortars and medium machine-guns in headquarters company, the 'carrier' platoon; so named because it consisted of six Brens – later, 12 – each mounted in a lightly armoured tracked vehicle. At about the same time, a light mortar, firing high explosive and smoke bombs of 2-inch calibre, was brought into service for the carrier and all rifle platoons, though many regular soldiers had never seen such a weapon before the outbreak of war in September, 1939. Similarly, the 0.55-inch Boys anti-tank rifle was officially in service but known only to many battalions by report when mobilisation began. An even more advanced weapon, a towed anti-tank gun, firing a solid 2 pound shot, was undergoing service trials.

A catalogue of weapons may seem out of place as the first item in an account of infantry tactics; but the fact is that, while man was and is the most important influence on the battlefield, the nature of that influence depends in substantial measure on the weapons and equipment available to him. This is particularly true for the infantryman, some of whose number are always in contact or potential contact with the enemy in all forms of war, by day or night in all weathers. Of all the

A 3 inch mortar crew during an exercise in England in 1940. The 3 inch mortar had a range of about 1,300 yards and could fire smoke and H.E. bombs. The crew are armed with the No 1 SMLE rifle. They are carrying the mortar broken down into its tripod, base plate and tube while other men carry the bombs in three round fibre carriers.

The picture shows the emphasis on realism that came into training following the Battle of France and the evacuation at Dunkirk.

Highland infantry in an LCI (Landing Craft Infantry) fire Bren guns and Boys anti-tank rifles. Two of the Brens are fitted with the high speed 200 round anti-aircraft drum magazine.

military Arms, the skills required of the infantry are the most numerous and varied. Its members must be skilled in reconnaissance and sniping, in closing with the enemy in open country, woods or urban areas. They must be foremost in and the mainstay of the defensive line against enemy attack. They have a wide variety of weapons to man.

Unlike the other great armies in Europe, the British Army in 1939 was entirely professional, composed mainly of men engaged for seven years with the colours and five on the reserve. They were backed by part time volunteers, the Territorial Army. As in other Arms, it was possible to train the regular British infantry

much more comprehensively than their counterparts in the continental armies. Each infantry regiment had its own depot at which it trained recruits in basic skills: drill, weapons, fieldcraft, map reading, and minor tactics based on the twin principles of fire and movement. A well-worn analogy was popular among instructors to illuminate the latter: 'Be like the parrot climbing up the cage: always have one leg in position before you take the next step. If the riflemen are moving, the light machine-gun should be on the ground in action. If the Bren is moving, the riflemen should be down ready to fire to give it cover.' Men were brought at depots to a mean standard of physical fitness to march 20 to 30 miles a day in full equipment and carry out bayonet practice on straw dummies at the end of it. Fortunately, by 1939, a new uniform was being introduced for the field, 'battledress', consisting of a blouse in place of the service dress jacket with its brass buttons, and loose trousers with ample pockets, trouser bottoms being confined in web anklets round the tops of the excellent quality leather boots. The old broad webbing equipment introduced in 1908 was also giving way to a modified, lighter model which included pouches specially designed to accommodate spare magazines for the Bren. Indeed, from 1937 onwards, the policy of rearmament and re-equipment gave promise of opportunities to the British infantry to develop their tactical expertise to exceptional standards of proficiency. But in the months remaining before the war, funds were insufficient to provide either the additional ammunition or the land for field firing exercises necessary for their realisation.

The consequence was that the British infantryman was well trained as an individual – ammunition was just sufficient to sustain individual skills – but had little practice in collective tactics in his platoon or company, and none in the application of fire outside the

British soldiers firing a 2 inch mortar at a house in which a sniper has been located. This mortar has a sight fitted at the base of the tube. Later marks had a white stripe painted down the barrel and the operator relied on his eye and judgement of distance to place the bombs on the target. With practice this could be done with a fair degree of accuracy.

strict artificial limits of the gallery range. Similarly, the training of the regimental officers was limited. The younger officers were influenced by the practical knowledge of their seniors acquired during the World War I. Though many of these seniors themselves recognised the need to throw off the constraints of the trench environment, and all exercises theoretical or practical were related to 'open' warfare, the weight of experience derived from the fact that the greater part of the British Army had been engaged intensively in France and Flanders for more than four years led to a deliberate approach to all tactical policies, a model sustained by the lessons of campaigning over the years on the north west frontier of India. Operations were deemed to fall into four phases: the advance; the deliberate attack; the defence; withdrawal. While tactical manuals advised that none of these phases should be taken in isolation, they were in practice studied as separate activities principally as a matter of convenience. One of the 'phases of war' was often the subject of study and exercise over a training year.

An attempt was made in 1937 to prepare the British Army for modern warfare by publication of a new manual of *Infantry Training – Training and War* as it was sub-titled – and the chapters attempted to marry the

A 3 inch mortar in action in North Africa. It had a rate of fire of about ten rounds a minute. With rapid fire these could be in flight simultaneously.

that 'mobile troops' – armoured cars and/or light tanks – would precede the infantry advanced guards as the horsed cavalry had once done. In the event of contact, battalion commanders were to be ready 'to assist the mobile troops in dealing with minor opposition, and commanders of advanced guard battalions should be prepared to move forward without delay so that plans can be made and put into action at short notice.' Then, 'as contact is gained, infantry units will deploy on a wider front, companies making full use of tracks and cross-country lines of advance. . . Time will be of the utmost importance. . . Reconnaissance groups must therefore be immediately available.' Guidance was given as to the combined action of infantry and tanks when the latter were deployed in cooperation, though no suggestions were made as to how the marching infantry could match the pace of the mobile troops. They either fell behind or held the latter back. Because there had been so few joint field exercises, the problem was not manifest.

Still, errors and omissions apart, the principles enunciated in the manual were thoughtful and practical. The spirit of quick reaction to contact was stimulating. But the shadows of World War I could not be kept out; there was always the expectation of a deliberate attack as the only means of breaking the main enemy position. 'In such cases,' the manual warned, 'to attack by day with any hope of success without excessive casualties requires deliberate and methodical preparation. . .' The same influence pervaded instructions for the defence. Neither the more general *Field Service Regulations* nor *Infantry Training* had advanced significantly from 1914. On being ordered to defend a point or area, platoons, companies or battalions selected ground offering cover from view and observation over the enemy and then dug in to obtain cover from fire. Initially, each man dug an

best of the old principles of open warfare learned in South Africa or on the Indian frontier with those which were expected to obtain as a result of the growing capability of tanks and armoured cars.

In the advance to contact, it was expected

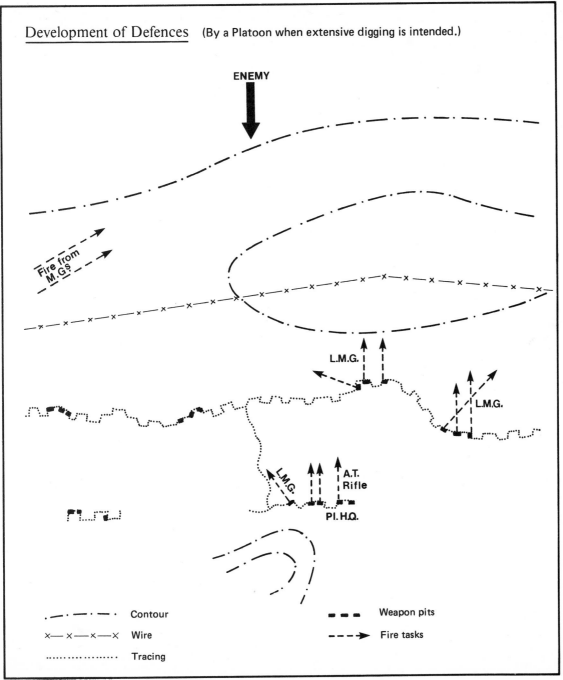

Development of Defences (By a Platoon when extensive digging is intended.)

ENEMY

Fire from M.Gs.

L.M.G.

L.M.G.

L.M.G.

A.T. Rifle

Pl. H.Q.

—·—·—·— Contour

—x—x—x—x— Wire

················· Tracing

▪▪▪ Weapon pits

--- ➤ Fire tasks

The layout of a platoon position as prescribed in the 1930s. Like World War I the Platoon has adopted a strictly frontal defence with weapons pits and tracings that conform to the pattern of the trench system. Though the machine guns to the left flank give some cross fire there are no linked arcs of fire within the platoon.

Private A. Jones and Pte. Renwick of the Durham Light Infantry in a weapons pit. They have an 18 set man pack radio. In the foreground is the signaller's Sten gun. Items of 38 pattern web equipment can be seen on the edge of the trench.

artillery and mortar fire on trench lines. Cover from fire, they believed, was more important than cover from view if the choice had to be made.

It is of interest that the diagrams which supported the defence doctrine show even more strongly the old trench warfare mentality: for example, medium and light machine-guns were sighted on forward arcs on the assumption that the enemy would always be obliged to assault frontally. Developed fully, the defences repeated the pattern of those carried across Flanders and France from 1915 onwards. This did not train the army to meet the most likely threat; for the German concept was to break through on a narrow front with heavy fire power as a preliminary to passing numbers swiftly through the gap or gaps made to attack the foe in flank and rear.

Fortunately for the British and French, German industrial capacity was unable to cope with the high and complex demands made upon it for the re-equipment of the renascent army. In 1936, the equipment programme was designed for deployment of 63 armoured divisions by the end of 1939. Progress was so limited by the beginning of 1938 as to necessitate a review. A senior officer of the operational requirements department, Oberst von Schell, revised radically the immense list of items on demand, largely by simplifying and rationalising a number of systems. The new programme aimed to produce essential requirements for 12 armoured divisions by the end of 1939, and might have achieved this but for the necessity of replacing losses in the Polish campaign. Thus the actual number of armoured divisions deployed on 1st January, 1940, was ten. Each of these contained a brigade of infantry mounted at first in modified civil trucks but later in specially designed half-tracks (the Sd Kfz 251). These brigades were particularly strong in automatic weapons and mortars roughly corresponding in calibre to those used by the British.

individual pit for himself and his weapon or, in the case of the medium machine-guns and 3-in mortars, dug with other members of the crew a pit for their particular support weapon. So far, so good. But, 'There will be a danger to the defence if trenches stand out as isolated entities, as the enemy will then be able to deduce not only the location but also the strength of the garrison. This can best be overcome by rapid and extensive digging between platoons and company localities in both the forward and reserve areas, though cover from ground observation will still be attempted. . .' The men who wrote this manual had not forgotten the cruel punishment of

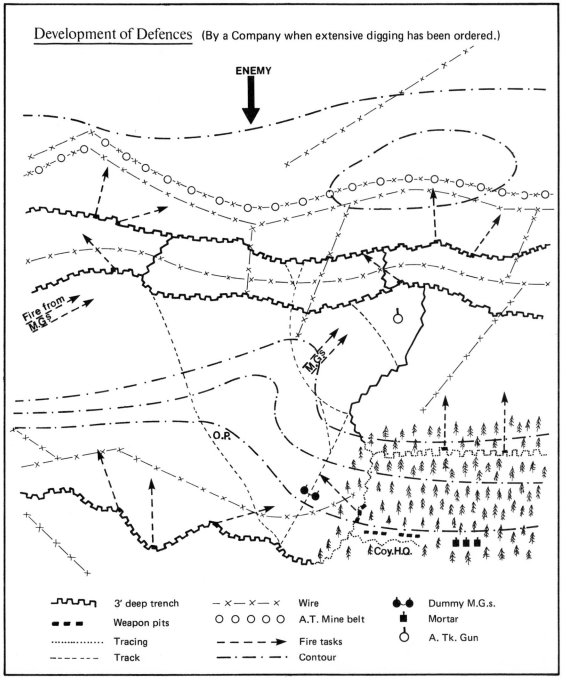

Development of Defences (By a Company when extensive digging has been ordered.)

ENEMY

Fire from M.G.s

M.G.s

O.P.

Coy.H.Q.

ᴖᴖᴖᴖ	3' deep trench	— ×—×—×	Wire	●●	Dummy M.G.s.
▰ ▰ ▰	Weapon pits	O O O O O	A.T. Mine belt	▰	Mortar
··············	Tracing	— — —▶	Fire tasks	⊖	A. Tk. Gun
— — —	Track	—·—·—·	Contour		

A Company position in the 1930s. The platoon position on page 11 is in the top right corner. The tracing has been extended into a trench system, a second line has been dug and communication trenches extended back to the final line around the Company H.Q. With the addition of belts of barbed wire the position has taken on all the appearance of a World War I trench line.

13

German infantry hitch a ride on a PzKpfw III F during the invasion of the Balkans in 1941. Taking infantry into action on tanks meant that they could deploy quickly to attack anti-tank guns, but if the tank was ambushed casualties could be very heavy.

Home defence troops apart, the greater number of field forces in the German Army were, however, disposed in infantry divisions, whose battalions relied on sea or rail transport for strategic movement, and their feet for tactical movement. Their supporting transport was horse drawn from first to last throughout the war. The role of these forces was to follow the armoured and motorised formations to hold the ground they had taken, and to round-up disorganised elements remaining in the original main battle zone.

The position at the outbreak of war, then, was as follows: the Germans had developed a strategic concept – *blitzkrieg* – the aim of which was rapid and complete victory. The role of infantry in this was limited, but nonetheless important. The motorised infantry, moving among or close to the tanks, were to be ready to dismount into action whenever the armour was held up by anti-tank weapons sited in cover, attacking their crews by a process of infiltration from one or another flank, helped forward by their own mortars, directly observed tank fire and whatever air and artillery sources were immediately available. The practice of extensive reconnaissance, exhaustive orders and a deliberate attack dependent

upon formal fire planning was forbidden. The motorised infantry were expected to emulate the armour by use of shock action. As a means of fostering this policy, an important change was made in the tactical training of infantry officers. Where, previously, during tactical studies in the field without troops, the directing staff had posed the problem and then given students an hour to reconnoitre and reflect, from 1937 onwards the problem was posed and, within a few minutes, a student would be called on at random to give his solution. When perhaps two or three had been heard, the group director would take the students through the several plans to see how they would have worked out. Whatever criticisms might have been offered, none were made to discourage dash. In the British and French Armies, the former method continued.

German motorised infantry were also taught to apply the principle of quick reaction to overcoming opposition to the advance on minor routes or those running through close country when a panzer grenadier regiment might be leading. It was impressed similarly on the parachute and gliderborne infantry of Student's airborne formations; for although these troops belonged to the Luftwaffe, their

An SdKfz 251/1 half track infantry carrier in Russia drives past a burning BT7 tank. The SdKfz 251 could carry twelve men, the driver, commander and ten men in the infantry section. The vehicle in the photograph has been fitted with six frames, three on each side, to take 28 cm H.E. or 32 cm incendiary rockets.

15

officers and non-commissioned officers were soldiers in origin.

It was, of course, foreseen that from time to time the offensive momentum might be slowed – even temporarily halted – by obstacles such as deep minefields or demolitions which could not be by-passed. These were expected to be covered by enemy infantry and anti-tank fire. To protect the engineers at their work of clearance and equally to ensure quick resumption of movement when routes were opened, the German motorised infantry were expected to mount a strong attack directly off the line of march. A battalion was trained to mount such an operation, including regimental support elements, on a 600 yard front in about 40 minutes from the moment of the point striking the obstacle to the assault. The commander would plan and execute the operation on the same set of principles guiding his subordinates in their smaller scale attacks. The simple rule was to win the fire fight (*Feuerkampf*) by establishing progressively fire superiority on the frontage of attack to whatever depth circumstances demanded. Three phases were involved.

1 The foremost troops, up to a company in strength with support from mortars and heavy machine-guns, would engage in pinning down (*niederhalten*) the enemy, forcing individuals in each set of defences under cover away from fire positions. This activity also helped to cover the brief reconnaissances of assault commanders, and the deployment of assault bodies.

2 As the latter infiltrated forward, fire elements would engage also in blinding (*blinden*) the defence while simultaneously maintaining offensive fire.

3 Finally, (*niederkampfen*), beating down the enemy with intense fire would be undertaken by all elements involved: mortars and machine-guns on to flanks and rear of the defensive position; assault elements into

the heart of the sector selected for destruction.

Now, it might be reasonably remarked that this concept was simply a development of the established principle of fire and movement, and very similar to that taught by the British – and indeed the French – to their infantry leaders. The first would be true, the second would not. Wherein lay the difference?

The German concept confined the attack to a narrow frontage, required the attacking commander to concentrate all his fire resources in this narrow sector, expected as a matter of course that the flanks would be engaged by the tanks or light armour, and the rear by artillery fire and ground attack aircraft arranged by the regimental staff. This dispensed with the delays involved in consultation and preparation of a comprehensive fire plan involving a number of elements. Time was thereby gained.

Then, as in the smaller scale actions, reconnaissance was kept to a minimum, assault troops were neither formed up nor kept to the steady pace of a linear advance as they moved in small groups by infiltration.

Of course, this method left more to chance, risked misunderstandings between those firing from one point, those from another so that the attackers were occasionally shot by their own side's fire, or by the enemy from areas of the defence neglected. But the German view, subsequently justified by their successes in 1940, was that these casualties were appreciably lighter than those to be suffered by the old deliberate methods which allowed the

German troops, one equipped with a Model 35 flame thrower, assault a Russian bunker.

enemy to establish fire initiative. It is no wonder that the French, who had come to believe in the supremacy of defensive weapons in the field, and the British, who maintained a belief in the unfolding of an operation by deliberate stages, were caught off balance as much by the speed and aggression of the German motorised infantry as by the tanks they supported in the early summer of 1940. The host of survivors from the defeat who reached British shores contained men determined to abandon the old methods of fighting as infantry.

Dunkirk post-mortem

Of all the Arms preparing to resist invasion that summer and autumn of 1940, the infantry was the strongest; and the greater part of the infantry had not been to France or Belgium. There was a handful of regulars, a mass of Territorial Army battalions, the swelling increment of national servicemen, and the newly formed Local Defence Volunteers, soon to be renamed Home Guard. It would not be easy to inculcate new ideas quickly among so many.

The appointment of General Sir Alan Brooke as commander-in-chief, Home Forces, with his chief-of-staff, General Sir Bernard Paget, did much to accelerate change. A small panel of officers was selected to develop new tactical ideas for the infantry. As these began to take shape, it was decided also to use a brisker style of English and cartoon style of illustrations in their presentation. Perhaps a greater innovation, the basic lessons of the new method were to be taught as a drill. To allay the fears of those who apprehended a return to fighting in 'squares', the opening address to instructors at the first of the new 'battle schools' contained these words:

'We are not proposing either to return to the tactics of the Peninsular War nor to abandon the principles which the Germans have shown us to be applicable still. Our aim is to teach the basic ploys so that they are second nature to every infantryman. Then the leaders – junior and senior – can develop their own ideas and methods. We'll give you the theme; you provide the orchestration. . .'

The scope was not quite as wide as that; it was, after all, necessary to have common

A British officer with a Thompson Model 1928 A1 sub-machine gun in the summer of 1940.

Norwegian troops with a Vickers medium machine gun in 1940. The Vickers was already 57 years old in 1939, but it was a reliable and much respected weapon. It remained in service with the British Army until 1961. It had a rate of fire of 450 to 550 r.p.m., was fed by a 250 round canvas belt and had a range of up to 2,000 yards. The water cooled barrel required 7½ pints and a condenser was fitted to hide and recoup the steam.

tactics for the infantry as a whole. But this form of approach encouraged initiative among the officers and non-commissioned officers in infantry battalions on whom the burden of leadership and instruction fell. It enthused the majority.

The first stage of instruction involved convincing trainees that battles were won by the action of small parties, platoons – even sections or detachments – which continued fighting when cut off from higher directions or supply. It was made clear that this applied as much in offence as defence. The prospects of success and survival would be the greater, it was contended, if all the members of such an isolated body knew what to do in basic situations such as coming under fire, or moving yet maintaining all round observation;

and knew also what others in the group would be doing to the point of being able to rely on it.

Thus the first drill began. The rifle section would form up on the barrack square and on command from the instructor each individual would call out his individual task.

'Section commander,
'No 1 on the Bren (light machine-gun),
'No 2 on the Bren,
'Section 2iC (second-in-command),
'No 1 rifleman – sniper,
'No 2 rifleman – bomber,
'No 3 rifleman
'No 4 rifleman – rearguard.'

Next would come the command: 'Observe!' Each man would turn to the arc allotted to his task, sufficient overlap being allowed over the

Drill for the Assault

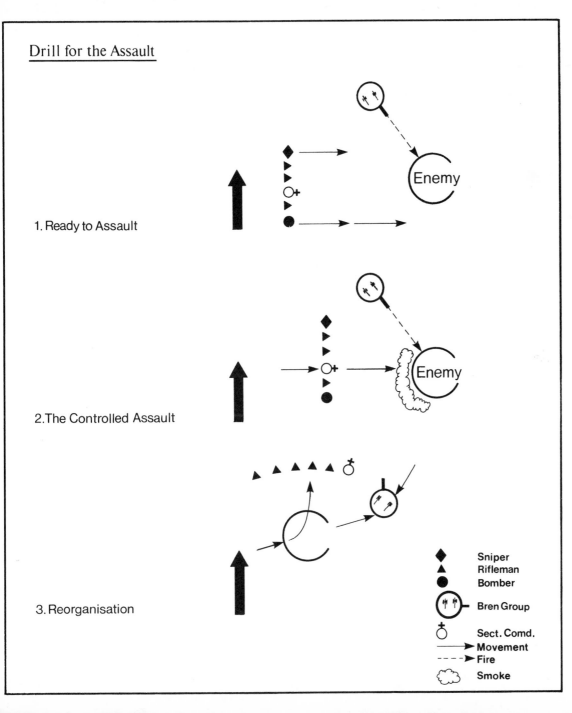

1. Ready to Assault

Enemy

2. The Controlled Assault

Enemy

3. Reorganisation

♦ Sniper
▲ Rifleman
● Bomber

⊘ Bren Group

⚲ Sect. Comd.
→ Movement
---▶ Fire
☁ Smoke

The drill for assault. The section commander sends his light machine gun off to the flank to keep the enemy's head down as the section deploys for the attack. As it closes with the enemy smoke grenades are used to blind the position and then the section goes through with the assault. They regroup beyond the position. This prevents enemy artillery and mortars firing on the known map reference of the position in the hope of catching the section regrouping after the assault. A section would not attempt to attack anything stronger than a small group of riflemen. Destroying a machine gun post was the job for a platoon.

The section covers both sides of the road so that they can see anyone dug in along the hedge row and also present less of a target if they are ambushed. The rear man has a vital task since the section could be shadowed by an enemy patrol who would wait for a favourable moment to spring an ambush.

Night Patrols

A section advancing along a road.

Leading Group	1. Section commander leads the patrol.
	2. Watches right.
	3. Watches left.
Right Group	4. Watches his front, the leading group and leader's signals.
	5. Watches right.
Left Group	6. Watches the leading group and leader's signal.
	7. Watches left.
Rear Man	8. Watches the rear.

360 degrees to take account of casualties. The section would then begin to advance, suiting its formation to the ground described by the instructor, close or open countryside, urban street, whatever was to be practised. Shortly, the instructor called, 'Under fire!' The section would shout in unison, 'Down – crawl – observe – take-up fire position!' suiting the actions to the words. The section commander would then be required to call out orders to execute his tactical plan, somewhat on the following lines:

'Left flanking – Bren take up fire position there: riflemen give covering fire. Bren group (in position), give covering fire by observation. Remainder, follow me.' This was a major advance on the deliberate though otherwise excellent teaching enshrined in *Infantry Section Leading, 1938*.

Platoons drilled collectively in the same way, though a platoon commander had the option of performing a pincer movement in addition to flank attacks right or left. Though necessarily slightly fuller, his orders were still very brief. For example, for the pincer movement conducted during the second stage of training, away from barracks and in the countryside, the sequence of events and orders might be:

1 Platoon moving forward – point (leading) section comes under fire.
2 Point section goes to ground, tries to get forward by fire and movement but finds weight of enemy fire too heavy.
3 Platoon commander (who is immediately behind point) observes strength and orders section commander: 'Stop! You will be fire section.' Section commander begins moving

A section advancing along a hedge or the side of a wood.

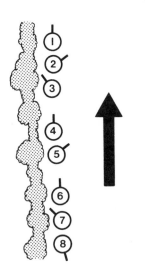

1. Section commander leads the patrol.
2. Watches right flank.
3. Watches left flank.
4. Watches the leading group.
5. Watches right flank.
6. Watches the group in front.
7. Watches left flank.
8. Watches the rear.

The section adopts a single file formation with the section commander leading. Each member of the patrol has his 'arc of responsibility' the area he would watch while on the move and when the patrol haults. During longer delays they would adopt a position of all round defence.

individuals into best positions to fire at enemy.

4 Platoon commander sends his runner to fetch the other two section commanders to a rendezvous. Meantime, he makes a quick reconnaissance based on the following: a. a quick look at the ground will usually yield more than a map study. b. a quick look at either flank will suffice if you know what you are looking for: clear lines of advance. Don't waste time looking for the best; something less will do. c. don't guess at what you can't see. Use your map to get an idea of the ground beyond your observation.

5 The platoon O (for Orders) group has arrived; that is, platoon sergeant, section commanders and No 1 on the 2-inch mortar and anti-tank weapon. Orders are:

'Enemy 400 yards in area of that barn. We will destroy the enemy there.
Pincer movement: Fire section – No 1. Left flank – No 2. Right flank – No 3. Anti-tank – fire with No 1 section. Mortar – HE as we move forward to flanks.
All support fire to continue until we come into view.
I will travel with 2 Section. Platoon sergeant remain here. Signal for assault one red Verey (cartridge) over 3 Section. Questions? Move!'

6 The platoon moves into position by infiltration along enemy flanks; the assault is made. Sections do not then need further instructions as to general areas in which to take up temporary defence; this is part of the drill. They will thus draw away spontaneously from the objective they have just

British paratroops and Commandos near the Normandy beaches in June 1944. The paratroops are armed with Sten guns while the Lance Corporal has a Colt 45 pistol.

cleared so as not to be in danger of enemy artillery or mortar fire on a known position, and will only need readjustment if they are to remain in defence for any significant period. (See also plates on pages 48-54).

There were drills for defence as well as the advance and quick attack; for cooperation with tanks; for the breaching of obstacles; for patrolling. All these began with the section,

irrespective of the fact that a section rarely operates on its own: the idea was maintained that if it is on its own it will continue operations independently. Even the platoon was scarcely viable against more than an enemy section in prepared defences. The sub-unit capable of semi-independent operations for any period of time was the rifle company. At this level, and that of the battalion to which

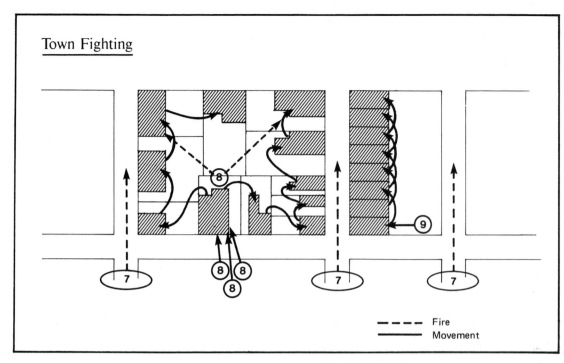

Town Fighting

⑧ ⑧ ⑧ ⑧ ⑦ ⑨ ⑦ ⑦

- - - - - Fire
———— Movement

A Company house clearing operation. While 7 Platoon keeps the streets covered 8 Platoon captures one house by frontal assault and then clears the rest through back windows while its Bren guns give cover. Nine Platoon 'leap frogs' down a row of terraced houses on the right. Houses were cleared by breaking through the roof and working down through the floors.

Below: British troops in training. (See also plate page 40).

it belonged, the contradictory demands for speed of reaction and time for reconnaissance, planning, orders, coordination of fire support, movement and assault were felt acutely. Sloughing off old attitudes was the more difficult because umpires on exercises were often officers dedicated to the old school of deliberate preparation, and they were often able to find evidence to support the criticism, more haste less speed.

Company commanders had to learn how to reconnoitre and make judgements on the move much as their platoon commanders were obliged to do. Time was saved by taking the artillery forward observation officer attached on reconnaissance and the mortar and other supporting fire controllers, even though the 'R' (reconnaissance) group became somewhat bigger than was desirable as a consequence. 'Dry' training – drills – were used

The British Rifle No 1, Mark III, Short Magazine Lee Enfield, 0.303 inch. The SMLE which was adopted for service in 1902 saw at least six modifications, the latest being the weapon illustrated. It had a ten round detachable box magazine, a muzzle velocity of 2,440 fps and a range of up to 1,000 yards, though the effective range was between 200 and 500 yards. It had a 16 inch long sword bayonet which weighed 1½ lb.

The Sten sub-machine gun Mark II. The Sten weighed 8 lb with a full magazine of 32 9 mm rounds. It had sights set for 100 yards, but the effective range was about 75 yards. Its muzzle velocity was 1,170 fps. A crudely made gun it was cheap and simple, but the magazine feed made it prone to jams. The soldier in the illustration would receive a nasty shock if he fired the gun as the fingers of his left hand are over the ejection port of the weapon.

British soldiers clearing houses in Colle, Italy. The man kicking in the door is holding a grenade ready to throw into the house.

how to take advantage of tank fire power and mobility while supporting the tank troop, were able to undertake enterprising tactical ventures. One serious weakness persisted, however: apart from the motor infantry battalions established in armoured divisions, the British infantry were otherwise limited still to their marching pace, and thus the tanks were held back to this speed.

Battalion commanders had to adapt their tactics to new weapons coming into service. Until 1940, commanding officers were accustomed to lay out their defensive positions in conformity with the siting of their medium and light machine-guns, the principal sources of fire. In the western desert, however, on rolling ground almost devoid of cover, battalion positions were necessarily sited to deny tank approaches. The defences were thus laid out on the commanding officer's organic anti-tank guns rather than his machine-guns; and increasingly his ground options were limited as brigade commanders were obliged to lay out their formations on the Royal Artillery regiment or battery of anti-tank guns allocated to them. Infantry anti-tank weapons would then be superimposed on this structure. The aim was not simply to knock out tanks attempting to force a way through the forward defences but also to prevent enemy tanks from standing off and, with their fire power and protection, picking off the infantry positions at will.

In the desert and, later in Europe, the basic defensive position for the infantry had stabilised at the two or four man slit trench. No attempt was made to connect trenches. Where possible, overhead cover was erected, and if the soil or revetments permitted, the occupants scraped sleeping places for themselves in the walls. Such tiny positions, though by no means invisible from the air, were not so easy to pick up as full trench complexes. They were often impossible to see from the enemy lines,

even at this level in some battalions to work out the best procedures. All battalions exercised regularly together to develop them comprehensively. When tanks were involved, battalions which had practised what became known as 'Second Echelon' drills with the armour at section and platoon level, learning

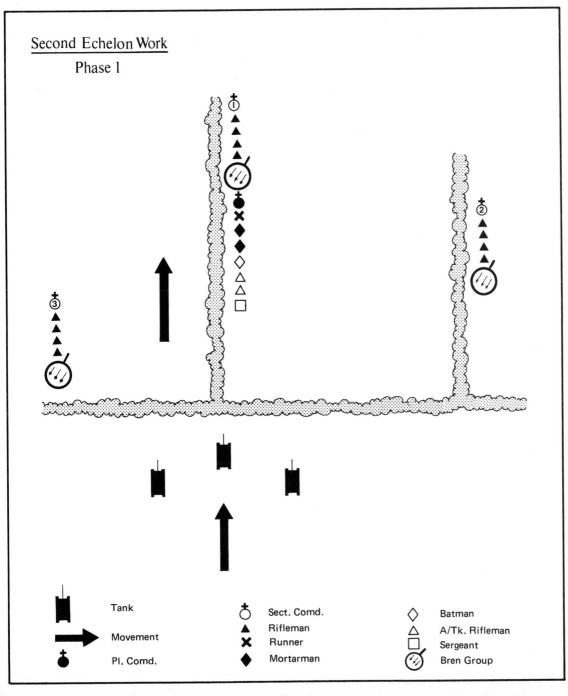

Second Echelon Work

Phase 1

A Platoon advancing with one section up and a troop of tanks in support. The infantry are using cover and searching the ground for indications of the enemy. The platoon is in a rough triangle with the commander in the headquarters section.

Tank	Sect. Comd.	Batman
Movement	Rifleman	A/Tk. Rifleman
Pl. Comd.	Runner	Sergeant
	Mortarman	Bren Group

The Bren LMG Mark I. A 0.303 inch gas operated weapon, the Bren had a 30 round box magazine and fired at 500 rpm. Developed before the war it weighed only 22.12 lb, could fire either semi or fully automatic and had a range of up to 2,000 yards. It had a quick change barrel which was essential since the gun was air cooled, and a trained man could fire 120 rounds a minute with four magazine changes.

The American M1 Garand rifle. A 0.30 calibre gas operated semi automatic weapon, the Garand had an eight round non-detachable box magazine. It weighed 9½ lb had a muzzle velocity of 2,805 fps and an effective range of 550 yards. A simple and robust weapon the Garand became the standard infantry weapon for the U.S. Army, and by the end of the war almost exactly 4.2 million had been produced. The rifle could be fitted with a grenade launcher, bayonet or telescopic sight.

The platoon comes under fire and deploys to form a 'fire line' facing towards the enemy posts. The tanks start to move off to the flanks while taking the enemy under fire. In this sort of situation the platoon commander has to indicate the target and work out an attack plan. Some tank marks carried a telephone on the rear hull to permit such talk. Otherwise the tank troop commander had to get out or the platoon commander to clamber up and either exercise was hazardous when in action.

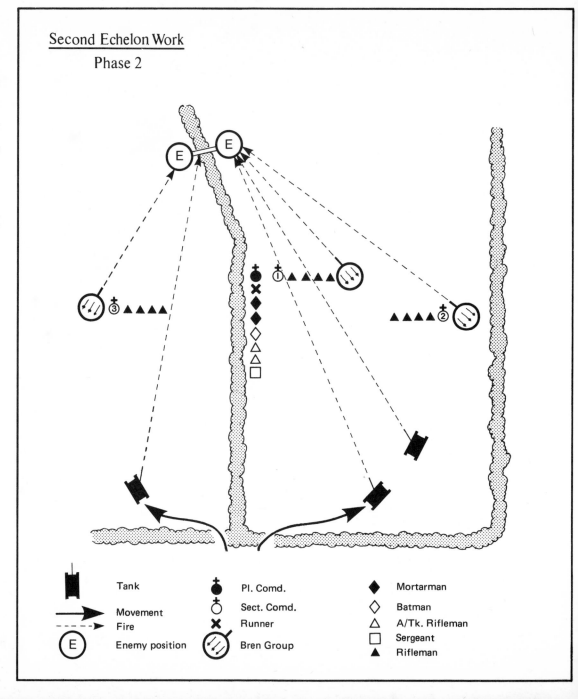

Second Echelon Work
Phase 2

🛡 Tank	⚥ Pl. Comd.	◆ Mortarman
→ Movement	○ Sect. Comd.	◇ Batman
⇢ Fire	✗ Runner	△ A/Tk. Rifleman
Ⓔ Enemy position	Ⓑ Bren Group	□ Sergeant
		▲ Rifleman

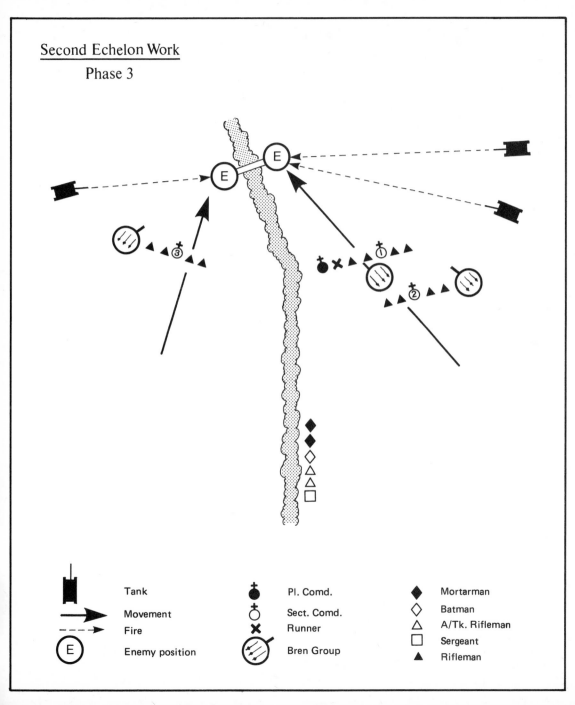

Second Echelon Work
Phase 3

In the final phase of the attack the tanks have moved to a position as nearly as possible at 90 degrees to the infantry. The infantry now assault and clear the enemy trenches while the tanks remain out of range of enemy grenades. Though these manoeuvres would be taught as a drill they would be adapted to suit the terrain and opposition as it was encountered.

Tank

Movement

Fire

E   Enemy position

Pl. Comd.

Sect. Comd.

Runner

Bren Group

Mortarman

Batman

A/Tk. Rifleman

Sergeant

Rifleman

The Browning Automatic Rifle M1918 A2. Known as the BAR this weapon had a 20 round box magazine and the A2 was capable of two rates of automatic fire either 500-600 rpm or 300-350 rpm. Its muzzle velocity was 2,650 fps and its effective range 800 yards. The weapon illustrated is missing its bipod which was attached near the muzzle. The British received 25,000 BARs after Dunkirk and allocated them to the Home Guard.

A Model 1928 A1 Thompson Sub-machine Gun. A 0.45 calibre weapon the Thompson had a 20 or 30 round staggered row detachable box magazine, or a 50 round drum. Though the rear sight was a leaf it also incorporated a notched battle sight seen in use in this illustration. The weapon had a muzzle velocity of 920 fps and a rate of fire of between 600 and 725 rpm, its effective range was 100 yards. The Thompson weighed 10¾ lb, but against this considerable weight it was reliable and robust.

though changes in light and temperature sometimes revealed for an hour or so what was hidden throughout the remainder of daylight. Whenever possible, defences were sighted on reverse slopes in open country, but it was only wise to do so when other points of observation offered the defenders warning of enemy approach and the means of bringing defensive fire down upon the intruders.

The abandonment of trench lines by the infantry was a relatively trivial outcome of the new approach to tactics. More important was the recognition of the need for an all round defensive capability by every body of troops in a battalion. It was an idea easier to understand and accept in theory than to practise, however. The human factor intervened. The main body of the enemy was known to lie in a certain direction; mines were laid, wire run in

Bersaglieri equipped with folding bicycles during pre-war manoeuvres.

Right: Italian troops with a Fiat 1914/35 8 mm machine gun. This gun could be used in an anti-aircraft role as well as ground use. It was not a good weapon and suffered badly from overheating.

lines which offered protection against an approach from that direction. Machine-guns conformed all too often, slit trenches being dug in such a way as to bring all three weapons in a platoon to bear on frontal arcs. It took many hard lessons to teach company and platoon commanders to maintain a potential for automatic weapon fire over 360 degrees and to interlock at least one of the arcs on each flank with those of the neighbouring sub-unit. The first of these measures provided the self-evident advantage of all round protection. The second promoted enfilade fire. A company, battalion, series of battalions which had interlocked their machine-guns medium and light across the defensive front and in depth behind it would almost certainly resist successfully the onslaught of an enemy three or four times as strong in infantry. Analysis of the break-in to any defensive position invariably shows that it was first achieved in an area where machine-guns were firing frontally. In such circumstances, they were vulnerable to the direct fire of the attackers and were, moreover, leaving open lanes between the streams of fire they poured out. Very similar principles applied to the sighting of anti-tank guns in

A ¼ ton Jeep in service with the S.A.S. in North Africa. It is armed with a single and a twin Vickers 'K' and a .5 inch machine gun. The Jeep provided infantry company commanders with the first form of cross country mobility since the horse in the 1920's.

The Russian 7.62 M1908 Moisin-Nagant rifle. This weapon was first adopted by the Russian army in 1891 and some six variants were produced before production ended in the late 1940s. It had a five round detachable box magazine, a muzzle velocity of 2,325 fps and a range of 600 yards. The M1944 model had a folding bayonet. The sniper model had a four power telescopic sight and the bolt handle was turned down flush alongside the body.

A DP (Degtyareva Pekhotnii) light machine gun. This weapon was designed in the early 1920s, it was gas operated with only six moving parts and weighed only 26 lb. It had a 47 round drum magazine, fired at 520 to 580 rpm and a range of 800 yards. The muzzle velocity was 2,770 fps. It saw action in the Spanish Civil War, and with modifications it is still in service as a belt fed LMG with Warsaw Pact forces.

A Company assault on a village. The Platoons avoid the streets which are covered by fire from 7 Platoon. The first group of houses are cleared by 8 and 9 Platoons. As one section covers the rear of the buildings the other one works through the houses. The third section has moved down to cover the road and isolate the houses so that they cannot be reinforced. When one block has been cleared the platoons move on to clear the rest of the village. Meanwhile 7 Platoon moves to isolate the village by positioning itself astride the road. In war these drills could be tailored to fit the situation, and house clearing in reality would take longer than it would in training. (See also plate on page 25).

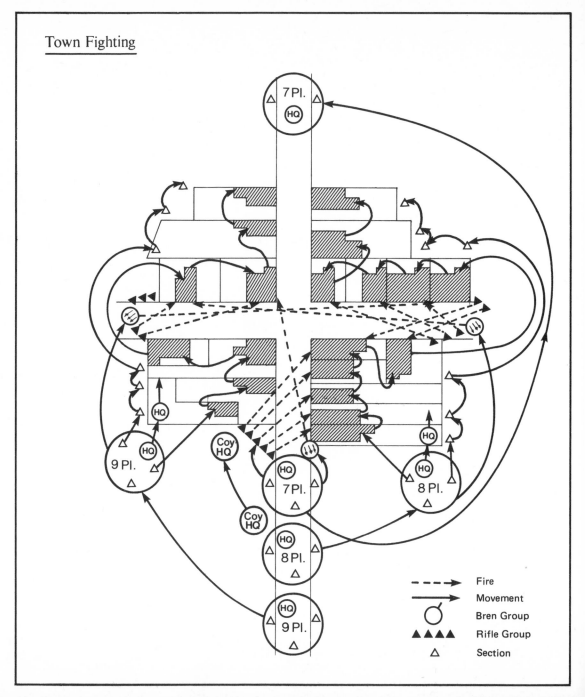

Town Fighting

Fire
Movement
Bren Group
Rifle Group
Section

defence; the same weaknesses opened the defence to attacking armour.

It was in the western desert that the British infantry first began to practise the art of mobile warfare. The campaign in 1940 was against the Italians who possessed good weapons and equipment but generally lacked the enthusiasm to make best use of it. Their tactics tended to be of the deliberate school, particularly in the infantry, though rifle and light regiments had developed a number of procedures for quick attacks as a result of their experiences in Ethiopia. When the British turned to the offensive, their armour was supported by the motor battalions of the 60th Rifles and Rifle Brigade, travelling in Bren carriers and light trucks. Later, their mobility was to be improved by introduction of the United States' White half-track. But it was necessary to provide the remainder of the infantry with some form of transport and so selected brigades were progressively provided with an increment of trucks specifically for troop carrying. This was the origin of the lorried infantry brigade, the belated implementation of experiments tried briefly just before the war. It was the best Britain could do to make some of its foot soldiers mobile, a second best measure. The vehicles provided no protection against shell splinters or small arms attack and had a poor cross-country performance when the ground was rough or soft. The consequence was that the only infantry in the British Army which regularly used the quick attack off the line of march were those in the rifle regiments, supporting armoured brigades, and the parachute battalions. Still, the philosophy instilled, the techniques developed as a result of the new battle drills promoted a livelier approach to offence amongst the remainder to complement their traditional doggedness in defence. This was to pay its first dividends during the North African campaign in 1942.

In parallel, the Japanese infantry were teaching the British the value of the attack off the line of march, infiltration through close country and the surprise assault under cover of concentrated automatic and light mortar fire. Soon, battle drills for jungle fighting were being developed in the Far East.

The entry of the Japanese to the war had brought in also the United States of America. Meantime, as a result of German initiative, the Russians had joined the British in the struggle for Europe.

A 2 Pounder anti-tank gun on a portée mounting in North Africa. The 2 pounder could penetrate 40 mm of armour at an angle of 30 degrees at a range of 1,000 yards. It was used by both the Royal Artillery and the infantry.

The PPSh 41 7.62 mm sub-machine gun. The PPSh was a blowback operated weapon with either a 71 round drum or 35 round box magazine. It fired at 700 to 900 rpm had a muzzle velocity of 1,500 fps and an effective range of 150 yards. Though there were few machined parts principally the bolt and the barrel, the bulk of the weapon was stamped which made it cheap and quick to produce using semi-skilled labour.

The German Mauser Kar 98k rifle. This weapon had a five round fixed box type magazine, was bolt operated and had a range of 550 yards and a muzzle velocity of 2,265 fps. The Mauser bolt action was first produced in the 1880s and was notable for its great strength. Most models of the Kar 98k were capable of taking a bayonet and some were fitted with a grenade launcher.

The Red Army

The Red Army was no better prepared for war with first-class professionals such as the Germans than Britain or France had proved to be in 1940. This was already evident from the outcome of the Russo-Finnish war begun in November, 1939. Many weaknesses were then disclosed in leadership and staff work, in organisation, in standards of training including cooperation between Arms. The strength of the army lay in its numbers and hardihood. To these should be added, on the invasion of their land, an intense patriotism.

Of the 186 divisions of the field force in being in June, 1941, 110 were infantry. As a result of lessons learned in Finland, these had recently been reduced to a strength of 14,000. Among the transport, horses outnumbered motor vehicles. Each battalion included three rifle companies, 12 medium machine-guns, and a mixed platoon of anti-tank guns and mortars. Besides these marching troops there were small numbers of specialist infantry: some half dozen mechanised divisions included brigades of motorised infantry borne in trucks; a parachute force; and mountain formations.

The most striking differences between the German and Russian tactical doctrines in 1941 were that the latter stressed the need to attack always on as broad a front as possible – a view no doubt influenced by the numbers of infantry available – with the corollary that fire must mass also to cover the front. As a result,

no sooner had the advanced guard made contact than its members dug in to await developments. The training manual advised that:

'The commander of an infantry regiment (three battalions) normally arranges attacking battalions in two echelons, accompanying the second echelon himself, since it is upon the timely intervention of this latter that the success of the infantry attack depends. Close support is provided by the regimental artillery groups which frequently use direct fire methods. Additional artillery and infantry support tanks are provided from the division.

'After deployment, infantry units will take every opportunity of advancing by bounds at the double, or by crawling, with the object of getting nearer to the enemy and so reducing the distance to be covered when the order for the assault is given.'

In practice, each echelon advanced in line, whether tanks were cooperating or not. In the final stages of the assault, there would be a prolonged cheering, and those behind often began firing in the air simultaneously with the short range fire opened by those in the assault. In sum, offensive operations, even those of motorised troops, were deliberately mounted and tightly controlled.

In defensive warfare, in common with other armies, the infantry of the Red Army held the line. The expectation was that their own defences would be attacked in much the same way that they themselves intended to conduct

Left: Russian soldiers in a stylised picture of street fighting. They are armed with the 7.62 mm PPSh sub-machine gun and a Degtyarev DP light machine gun. The PPSh had a 71 round drum magazine, while the DP L.M.G. had a 47 round magazine.

The Maschinengewehr MG42. This weapon, the first general purpose machine gun, remains probably the finest gun of its type to be developed during the war. It weighed 25½ lb, and had the phenomenal rate of fire of 1,200 to 1,300 rpm. Feed was by 50 round belts and the muzzle velocity of 2,480 fps. The gun was designed to incorporate a large number of stamped parts and spot welds to keep down costs. It had an efficient barrel change which was essential since the gun was air cooled.

46

The MP40 sub-machine gun. A 9 mm blowback operated weapon the MP40 incorporated a number of improvements on the earlier MP38. It fired fully automatic at 500 rpm and had a muzzle velocity of 1,200 fps. The magazine held 32 rounds. Without the magazine it weighed 9 lb. The MP38 and 40 were notable as two of the first sub-machine guns to have folding stock. By the end of the war over one million MP40s had been produced by German and German controlled factories.

The Platoon is advancing with one section up and two back with the Platoon H.Q. The first section comes under fire and goes to ground. The Platoon commander calls an O Group with the section commanders of 2 and 3 sections and decides to outflank the position with a pincer movement. He then detaches the platoon sergeant and the 2 inch mortar and anti-tank rifle crews. The 2 inch mortar takes the enemy under fire while the Bren gun and riflemen of 1 section become the fire section. While the Platoon sergeant controls the fire the commander joins 3 section on the right flank.

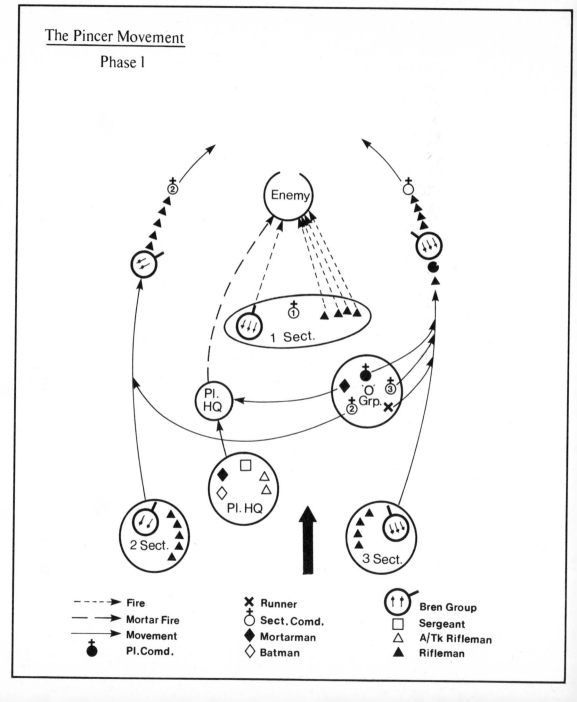

The Pincer Movement

Phase 1

In a pre-war exercise two Russian soldiers hunch behind their camouflaged 1910 Maxim machine gun. The Maxim was a tested and reliable weapon, but it was also very heavy. Fitted with its shield it weighed 99.71 lbs and the total weight was 152.5 lbs.

such operations. Thus the regulations ordered:

'Defences should be planned to counter superior enemy forces attacking simultaneously throughout the whole depth of the position and should aim at:

Destroying the hostile infantry in front of the foremost defended localities.

Preventing enemy tanks from breaking through beyond the enemy position.

In the event of a breakthrough by tanks, fragmenting their attack by anti-tank weapons, at the same time separating them from the accompanying enemy infantry by pinning down the latter with small arms fire. . .'

The infantry battalion anti-tank weapons were to be superimposed on the heavier calibres sited by divisional instructions, and themselves sited within and covering obstacles. Tanks were to be the principal counter-attack Arm except in close or mountainous country; but infantry regiments and divisions were to keep reserves to cooperate with them. Battalions and companies were to prepare for all round defence and to maintain it until relieved.

It is not clear whether withdrawal was practised as an accepted phase of war – some armies declined to recognise it in the belief that they might lead their officers to believe that withdrawal was respectable! Certainly,

German infantry in snow suits and whitewashed helmets on the Eastern Front in 1941. In the foreground are MG 34 machine guns with ammunition boxes.

ambushes were used during exercises, particularly when one side or the other was influenced to pull back. Whatever the facts, the Red Army spent many months in withdrawal following the German invasion. During this time, they learned by trial and error how to mount quick attacks at company level against any of the pursuing troops whose vigilance slackened. In the prolonged struggle to stabilise their line, they became expert in

urban warfare. During fighting in such cities as Stalingrad, storm groups were developed for quick local attacks, sub-units of up to 60 officers and soldiers armed with a high proportion of automatic weapons like the PPSH 7.62 mm sub-machine gun and including men who had become skilled bombers.

When the fortunes of war changed and the Russians began to push back, finally to pursue

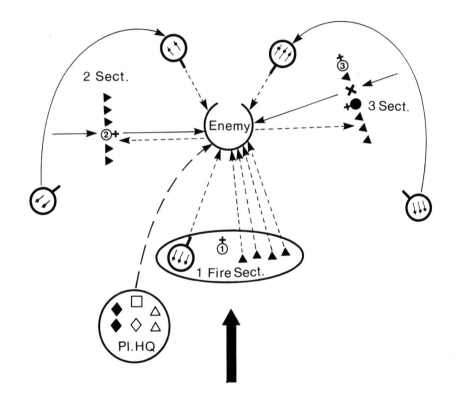

The Pincer Movement
Phase 2

2 Sect.

Enemy

3 Sect.

1 Fire Sect.

Pl. HQ

The enemy see the two sections moving round the flanks and start to fire at them. The section commanders detach their Bren guns who move off to positions on the flanks to act as cut offs should the enemy try to escape. The sections then prepare to move through the enemy position in an assault. The Platoon commander will have arranged a signal for the fire section to cease fire, but this will be timed so that the enemy are still under cover when 2 and 3 sections arrive in the position.

- - - - → Fire	✗ Runner	Bren Group
— — → Mortar Fire	⚲ Sect. Comd.	☐ Sergeant
—— → Movement	◆ Mortarman	△ A/Tk Rifleman
⬤ Pl. Comd.	◇ Batman	▲ Rifleman

their foe into Germany, two changes are evident in the practice of infantry tactics. The first and most notable was the cooperation between armour and infantry in the tank divisions and motor rifle divisions. Trucks had been introduced into many of these formations for the infantry and they had become adept at dismounting and deploying quickly to such tasks as clearing away enemy tank destroyers firing from defiladed positions. Anything stronger than this type of opposition, however, continued to result in the mounting of a formal attack with strong artillery support. Secondly, it had become a regular practice for Soviet infantry soldiers to travel in clusters on tanks where the the latter were operating with infantry divisions. It was a practice used often by the British and, yet more, the United States infantry as a means of keeping up with armour; and from time to time the poor judgement of commanders permitted their men to travel in this way in the vanguard with the result that they sustained heavy casualties in the first ambush they entered. But infantry of the Red Army certainly rode forward on tanks in the forefront of many battles up to the moment of their carrier opening fire in an engagement. Such events were remarked frequently in German battle reports. It was an expensive way of keeping infantry and tanks together but on several occasions at least it enabled the Russians to carry through with great success their policy of massed attack. Tanks with infantry aboard would appear and close up to the German defences despite heavy artillery, automatic and tank destroyer fire. On a signal, the infantry would dismount to begin their assault with customary cheers. The tanks moving in among them would be engaging targets. One German description of such an event concluded in this way: 'It was an unorthodox operation and a costly one, but it succeeded in driving us from defences in an hour and a half.'

Above Left: Russian infantry assault a bunker position.

Below Left: A Maxim machine gun crew in training bring their gun into action.

Above: German infantry in Russia await the order to advance during the winter of 1941.

Left: Russian Marines from the Soviet Northern Fleet serving as ground forces.

The re-groupment phase of the pincer movement. The sections have moved through the objective and men will have been sent back to check for maps and documents and wounded prisoners. The first section now moves to the flank and 2 section takes the point. The Platoon Sergeant would check the ammunition state and casualties. The radio operator would send back the Platoon commander's report of the outcome of the action. After the shock of the attack perhaps death or injury for friends in the platoon it would be a time for the officer to give quick word of encouragement before the platoon resumed the advance.

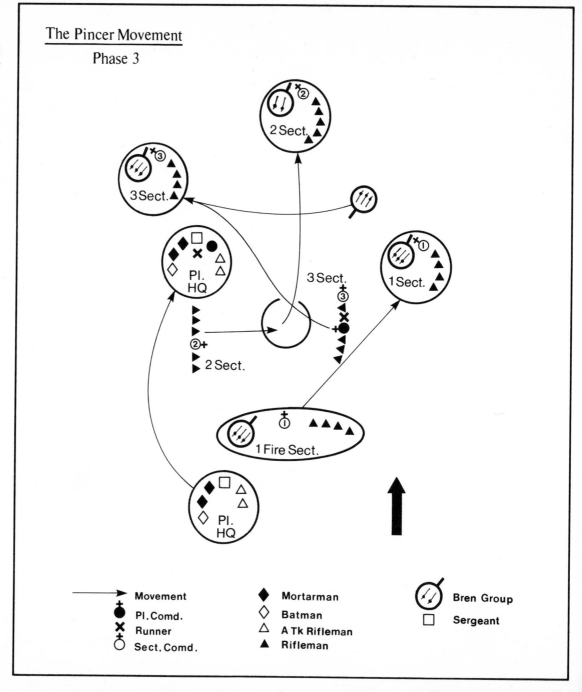

The Pincer Movement
Phase 3

2 Sect.

3 Sect.

Pl. HQ

1 Sect.

3 Sect.

2 Sect.

1 Fire Sect.

Pl. HQ

→ Movement	◆ Mortarman	Bren Group
● Pl. Comd.	◇ Batman	□ Sergeant
✕ Runner	△ A Tk Rifleman	
○ Sect. Comd.	▲ Rifleman	

Russian infantry their rifles and PPSh sub-machine guns at the high port double into an enemy held village.

Left: Recruit training for close combat. The men are learning how to parry a bayonet thrust with their entrenching tool.

Above: Russian cavalry at the charge. Though horses were at a severe disadvantage in mechanised war, cavalry could still work in swamps and forests.

Above Right: A Soviet engineer with a mine detector.

Right: In a pre-war exercise Russian soldiers ferry a light tractor and an anti-tank gun across a river.

Soviet soldiers manhandle a 45 mm anti-tank gun in marshy ground in central Russia. They are armed with 7.62 mm Moisin-Nagant rifles.

Below: An 82 mm mortar crew manpack their weapon during fighting in 1943.

The American Expansion

The Army of the United States of America began to expand in the months preceding the Pearl Harbour attack, changing at the same time its character from that of a professional to a conscript force. Although, inevitably, the infantry formed the strongest Arm, the proportion of infantrymen to others was somewhat lower than in the armies of the other major powers engaged in the war, a circumstance due to the demands on manpower by advanced technology, high mechanisation and a profusion of support weapon systems, great and small.

The enormous numbers involved in the expansion of American military forces after Pearl Harbour gave rise to many difficulties, not least in training individually and collectively the drafts of infantry officers and soldiers required to make good early casualties and to fill out the new divisions forming from the beginning of 1942 onwards. To reconcile huge classes and a scarcity of instructors, weapon training was often undertaken by a senior non-commissioned officer on a central platform surrounded by a class of perhaps 100 men whom he would take step by step through some aspect of the mechanism or handling, while two or three assistants would circulate to help those men obviously finding it difficult to follow instruction. Range practices were conducted on a system of batches passing through dedicated instructional staffs. A good deal of fieldcraft

was taught by lectures to large classes using cine films or other projections for the illustration of ideas and techniques. Much of the training of junior leaders was similarly theoretical. The burden of tactical training therefore fell to the new divisions, one they found equally difficult to discharge for lack of experienced commanders and staffs.

Manuals of minor tactics were published

Far Left: An American Lieutenant checks his map prior to an operation in 1944. The men are part of the First Allied Airborne Army, and though the censor has erased their divisional insignia they are probably men of the 82nd Airborne. The officer is armed with the M1 Garand rifle, while the Corporal has a .45 Colt in the holster on his web belt.

Left: An M3 Personnel Carrier – the famous 'White half track' during an exercise in the United States. Some 41,170 of these vehicles were built by Autocar, Diamond T and White. International Harvester also built some of the 70 different variants on this chassis.

Men of the U.S. 1st Army crouch behind their .30 Browning light machine gun during fighting in the streets of Aachen, Germany. The 1919 A4 Browning machine gun had an effective range of 900 yards and fired at 400 to 500 r.p.m.

which were not, in principle, dissimilar from the battle drill publications of the British Army. They were, however, much more comprehensive, embracing many more variations of situation and optional responses.

Three other influences should be noted on the tactics of the United States infantry. Organisationally, the regiment was the focus rather than the battalion; in this sphere the Americans were closer to the Germans than

the British. Technologically, their communications were superior to those of any other army at regimental level and below, their radios and telephones more widely distributed. There was thus a tendency to centralised control. Not least, there was the character of the American soldier, the product of an egalitarian society, 'determined', as a distinguished American military commentator has remarked of the infantry,

During fighting in Normandy an American soldier fires a 2.36 inch M1 anti-tank rocket launcher. Known popularly as the "bazooka" it had a range of 400 yards. The loader is taking cover on the left.

A soldier of the U.S. 9th Army aims his Browning Automatic Rifle up a side street during mopping up operations in Tangemunde, Germany. The BAR had a 20 round magazine and could fire either semi or fully automatic at 500 r.p.m.

Men of the 411th Infantry Regiment of the 103rd Division of the U.S. 7th Army clamber up a railway cutting during fighting in Alsace. They are armed with .30 M1 Garand semi-automatic rifles. In the centre is a man with the 2.36 inch rocket launcher and above him is a BAR rifleman.

Below right: Two U.S. soldiers show the rocket launcher M1 and M9. On the left is the early M1 a 54 inch long tube. On the right is the M9 which was lighter and could be broken down into two sections which then clipped together for easier carrying. At 13.25 lbs it was 1.20 lbs lighter than the M1.

'never to march a yard if there is a truck or automobile in sight. Willing to dig a foxhole if someone is likely to fire at him but just as ready to dodge behind a boulder. He was asleep in all the camouflage lessons. . .'

Even so, these same soldiers developed into veterans after a year or so, parachutists, armoured infantry – the first among the allies to perfect methods of fighting through light opposition from their half-tracks – and the men in the regiments of the many infantry divisions. The following illustrates well the adaptability of the latter, men of 26th Infantry fighting in Aachen in mid-October, 1944.

'In moving through the center of Aachen, Colonel Daniel's (3rd Battalion) men not only

Infantry of the U.S. 3rd Army pass through the suburbs of Metz during fighting in November 1944. The SCR-300 man pack radio carried by the operator on the right allowed patrols to report back their contacts with the enemy. The SCR-300 was the standard inter battalion radio and superior to equivalent in other armies of the day.

A 57 mm M1 anti-tank gun in the Belgian mud of December 1944. Based on the design of the British 6 pdr anti-tank gun the M1 had similar performance figures being able to penetrate 2.7 inches of armour at 1,000 yards.

A Sherman of the 7th Armoured Division advancing through the snow near St Vith in December 1944. This tank was used extensively with infantry as well as in armoured formations.

had to plow through the maze of rubble and damaged buildings in their path but also to maintain contact with Colonel Corley's (2nd Battalion) main effort against the northern hills. . . Colonel Daniel had an attack frontage of about 2,000 yards, no minor assignment in view of the density of the buildings. Of necessity, his advance would be slow and plodding.

'The fighting in Colonel Daniel's sector quickly fell into a pattern. Dividing his resources into small assault teams, (he) sent with each infantry platoon a tank or tank destroyer. These would keep each building under fire until the riflemen moved in to assault; thereupon the armour would shift fire to the next house. Augmented by the battalion's light and heavy machine guns firing up the streets, this shelling drove the Germans into the cellars where the infantry stormed them

A Tiger II crewed by men of the Waffen S.S. passes a column of American prisoners during the Ardennes Offensive. Behind it are two dispatch riders on 751 cc Zündapp motorcycles.

A patrol of the 8th Division US 1st Army moves cautiously to outflank a German sniper in Duren, Germany. The rocket launcher could be used to blast the sniper from his position while the rifleman kept his head down with small arms fire.

behind a barrage of hand grenades. Whenever the enemy proved particularly tenacious, the riflemen used the other weapons at their disposal, including demolitions and flame-throwers employed by two man teams attached to each company headquarters. The men did not wait for actual targets to appear; each building, they assumed, was a nest of resistance until proved otherwise. Light artillery and mortar fire swept forward block by block several streets ahead of the infantry while heavier artillery pounded German communications farther to the rear.

'To maintain contact between units, Colonel Daniel each day designated a series of check points based in street intersections and more prominent buildings. No sub-unit advanced beyond a check point until after establishing contact with the adjacent sub-unit. Each rifle company was assigned a specific zone of advance; company commanders in turn generally designated a street to each platoon.

'After a few bitter experiences in which Germans bypassed in cellars or storm sewers emerged in rear of the attackers, the riflemen soon learned that speed was less important than pertinacity. . . The men measured their gains in buildings, floors, and even rooms.'

One of the supporting tanks caught fire. '. . . a Company K squad leader, Sergeant Alvin R. Wise, rushed to the other tank to evacuate the wounded crew. The tank, he decided, might be recovered. Climbing inside, he began to spray adjacent German held buildings with fire from the tank's machine-guns. Under this

A Tank Destroyer moves through Brest during fighting in 1944. Tanks were often used to give direct fire support to infantry, and provided they were protected from enemy tank hunting teams they could be devastating in built up areas.

American troops fire an 81 mm mortar on an isolated German position near Nancy, France. The 81 mm mortar had a range of 3,290 yards and could fire two types of H.E. bomb, smoke and illuminant ammunition.

German soldiers with a 3.7 cm anti-tank gun during an attack near Kharkov in 1942. The gun could fire H.E. ammunition in close support role.

fire, two privates from (his) squad joined him in the tank. Though none of the three had ever been in a tank before, they somehow managed to start the motor, turn the tank around, and drive it down the street to safety.'

This brief glimpse of an infantry battle shows that the wheel had turned full circle.

The German infantry were on the defensive, short of experienced leaders due to casualties, their companies often made up to strength with inexperienced youths. The professional teaching of past days stood the survivors in good stead, however, even in this situation of reverse: the use of initiative by junior leaders;

Men of the Kings Shropshire Light Infantry recharge radio batteries. Behind them is a Universal Carrier part of the Battalion Signals platoon.

the continuous process of regrouping to meet changing circumstances; mounting of quick attacks whenever the enemy's attention wandered. But they could no longer triumph as the advancing and more numerous enemy had learned to practise the same lessons.

When the fighting came to an end in the following year, the infantry of both sides were still the basic fighting Arm in the combat zone as they had been at the end of the first world war. But their potential on the battlefield had expanded significantly and the British had put behind them forever the influence of trench warfare. It was not alone the early lessons of

An MG 34 machine gun crew with their weapon on its sustained fire tripod. The gun commander is on the right.

German *blitzkrieg* which had brought about the transformation.

Weapons technology had made many advances under the pressure of demand and these had extended to the infantry. The free-flight rocket launcher had come into service to counter tanks – the *panzerfaust* and bazooka were the most successful. The sub-machine gun, the German MP38/40 being the best of its type, had put automatic fire into the hands of the section to supplement the light machine gun. The quality and range of mortars and sustained fire machine guns had been greatly improved.

Then, radio communications had become a common feature of command and control in infantry battalions. A demand for a simple, robust, reliable – and cheap – radio for each platoon would have been laughed to scorn on Salisbury Plain in 1935. Ten years later, the British had emulated the Americans in the provision of such equipment. Yet, as an innovation, it was to prove a mixed blessing: the growth of ability to communicate to almost all points of the battlefield has tended to encourage centralisation of control and to tie senior commanders to their headquarters, to the detriment of personal command and the free play of subordinates' initiative.

Leadership in the infantry remained and still remains at a premium. At some stage in operations, the section, platoon, company, has to leave shelter and hazard itself in the open, whether on patrol, in an assault, in manning weapons to defend a position hotly engaged. The greater the risk of injury or death, the greater the need for leadership. Men do not obey an order in the heat of battle in mortal peril or a state of exhaustion because a man appointed formally to be their superior orders it. They obey only because they have confidence in the judgement and courage of the leader to carry them through the crisis. This burden lies heavily on the infantry junior leader due to the prolonged contact he experiences with the enemy, often in remote sites. In the end, it is probable that the outcome of battle depends more on this man than any other.

Infantry organisation guide

Formations

Division: 12-15000 men. All Arms formation including logistic units but main fighting element is (usually) three *brigades* or *regiments* of infantry.

Brigade: (British) 2,500-3,500 men. May contain all Arms. Main fighting element is (usually) three *battalions.*

Regiment: (French, German, Russian, United States)

Unit

Battalion: 650-800 men. Usually consists of three or four rifle companies, support or heavy weapons company, including:
    medium or heavy machine guns
    medium mortars
    medium anti-tank weapons
headquarters company including signals.

Sub-units

Rifle company: 100-180 men. Consists of three rifle platoons. May include a support weapons platoon.

Rifle platoon: HQ including light mortar and anti-tank weapon
Three rifle sections/squads (USA); each about 10 men and including
1-2 light machine guns
1 machine carbine/pistol
8 rifles